THE HANDY GUIDE TO

DIFFICULT AND IRREGULAR GREEK VERBS

Aids for Readers of the
Greek New Testament

✦

**Jon C. Laansma
Randall X. Gauthier**

Douglas S. Huffman
SERIES EDITOR

Kregel
Academic

The Handy Guide to Difficult and Irregular Greek Verbs:
Aids for Readers of the Greek New Testament

© 2017 by Jon C. Laansma and Randall X. Gauthier

Published by Kregel Publications, a division of Kregel, Inc., 2450 Oak Industrial Dr. NE, Grand Rapids, MI 49505-6020.

ISBN 978-0-8254-4479-1

Printed in the United States of America
17 18 19 20 21 / 5 4 3 2 1

Difficulties reveal heroes and cowards. Every war does precisely that. The Greek New Testament is a standing challenge to every preacher in the world.
~ A. T. Robertson

I have firmly decided to study Greek, nobody but God can prevent it.
~ Ulrich Zwingli

In so far as we love the Gospel, to that extent let us study the ancient tongues.
~ Martin Luther

It is no use for someone who wishes to be regarded as a specialist in the Bible to be in a position that he or she must take translations on trust.
~ F. F. Bruce

Paul wrote in an ancient language. That language only makes sense as koine Greek, understood in the light of the usage of koine Greek in the first century of the common era.... Anyone who tries to dispense with or to ignore the boundaries indicated by grammarian and lexicographer only confuses invention with understanding.
~ James D. G. Dunn

CONTENTS

PREFACE

The Handy Guide to Difficult and Irregular Greek Verbs: Aids for Readers of the Greek New Testament is a set of vocabulary aids for students of New Testament Greek. Its key contribution is a list of difficult verb forms (2nd–6th principal parts) in order of frequency of occurrence; the frequencies represent counts of all of the verbs (simplex + compounds) that share the same stem.

This learning aid resulted from classroom experience, in part through helping undergraduate students in Greek reading classes but also through watching graduate exegesis students struggle with the original language requirements of their programs. For many of the latter, their introduction to Greek had been the usual "three-and-out"— three semesters and then out into the wilds of detailed exegesis. After three semesters the language has usually been introduced but not yet *learned*. Nor will the practices of exegesis on their own do more than reinforce select and isolated features of the language. Reading ability will steadily decline unless there is a regular practice of reading. We are reminded of the advice of a weight lifter: If you want to lift heavy weights, you have to lift heavy weights. The missing step for many students of Greek is broad *reading*. It was the desire to assist in this step that most directly motivated the present text.

There are many published lists of the principal parts of the verbs of the New Testament (NT), but no list to our knowledge that records them in order of frequency of occurrence. Still less is there available a tabulation that counts the simplex stem together with its compounds under one frequency. Without frequencies, however, the beginning student has no way of knowing which stems merit special attention in the initial stages of learning. The simple (though hard-won) organization of these forms into frequency blocks should give students confidence that their time is being used efficiently. Likewise, an explanation of the morphological patterns that account for many of these "difficult" forms is helpful but dwarfs the list of the forms themselves; most students will never master these patterning principles nor retain them for ready use. What is more, many forms do not conform to any known pattern but are the result of the beautiful freedom of evolving human languages. We encourage the broader study of morphology but believe it might better be carried out while one is already *reading*.

The Handy Guide to Difficult and Irregular Greek Verbs as a set of aids for readers is not a matter of improving on an existing type of resource but of providing something new to add to those already available. Standard first year grammars, for instance, lay a foundation of principal parts of verbs. The most common stems are adequately covered. A closer look, however, will reveal that the stems drilled omit some that are in fact common in the NT and include stems that are very infrequent (perhaps occurring only 3–5x in the NT). This is because the usual approach is keyed to *lexical* forms. It does not account for compounds of irregular stems in particular, and it makes no attempt to prioritize irregular stems the way it does lexical stems. As a result, students who have been at work for two or three semesters have a mixed bag of tense stems—many on target, some out of the way, some just missing—with no way of improving their situation short of memorizing as many stems as possible regardless of frequency and/or constantly looking them up via parsing aids until they eventually "stick." The resource before you prioritizes the most relevant stems and then presents them in a straightforward list. This is not the only approach necessary to mastering the vocabulary of the NT, but it is a significant addition to time-tested strategies.

To avoid misunderstanding, it should be said immediately that the phrase "difficult and irregular" in this work reflects the perspective of a beginning student who takes the 1/s present indicative (lexical form) as the touchstone; it avoids further technical distinctions. We comment further on this in the "Note to Instructors and Interested Readers."

It is our hope that in time digital versions of this work could be made available that integrate with a tagged NT text and would offer additional ways to learn these stems, e.g., by calling up sentences that use particular stems or randomizing each frequency block with forms drawn from NT texts.

If the unruliness of many of the verbs in this list is appreciated, so also the difficulties of simplification. Hopefully our limited goal of providing a straightforward learning aid for beginning students will have been achieved.

To some the work required for such a list would seem frighteningly tedious. Can it be believed that friends would enjoy the labor of shared interests and the privilege of service?

The astute editorial eye of Alexa Marquardt removed several infelicities from our prose. The remaining problems are to be laid at our feet.

Thanks go to Kregel Academic, especially to Shawn Vander Lugt, Laura Bartlett, Paul Hillman, Dennis Hillman, and Herb Bateman, for editing and publishing this work; to Accordance for backing it at an earlier stage; to Douglas Huffman, Doug Penney, Dan Wallace, and Bill Mounce for their suggestions; to our families, especially our wives, for their support as we rummaged through these details; to our teachers for passing on their learning; to our colleagues for their fellowship in work worth doing; to our students for their eagerness to keep the tradition going and for their many questions.

INTRODUCTION

After a year or two of elementary Greek grammar the best thing a student can do is read, read, read. Turn off all parsing aids and close all interlinears. With a text and a print dictionary in hand, read, read, read. Read the Greek NT, the LXX, the Apostolic Fathers, Josephus, Epictetus, Aesop, Herodotus, and Homer. Much is learned through exposure. Of course, composition (English to Greek), too often neglected, is a key ingredient in gaining a degree of mastery. A time-tested complement to these exercises is simple vocabulary drilling, especially in the earliest stages, and for readers of the Greek NT helps like Bruce Metzger's *Lexical Aids for Students of New Testament Greek* have been standard.[1] It is only good sense to learn vocabulary beginning with the most frequently occurring words and proceeding in descending levels to the less frequently occurring words—all the while reading.

What is given herein is no substitute for these exercises but a further complement only. Anyone who has spent time struggling to make their way through the texts of the NT sooner or later observes that knowing all the lexical (1/s present indicative) forms in the world is of limited use if the verb has an irregular stem. What good is it to know that τρέχω is glossed *I run* if what one actually sees while reading is ἔδραμεν?

A further observation underscores this point. The verb αἱρέω occurs only 3x in the NT.[2] Its most common compound form, ἀναιρέω, occurs 24x. Because the separate forms occur so infrequently, many students may learn none of them in their course of study; and if they dip low enough into a list of lexical forms to reach ἀναιρέω, they will learn only the *lexical* stem. The form of this verb most often encountered is the 3rd principal part (PP), -εῖλον [-ελειν].[3] Since that is what the students will see, they will be stumped. It is an irregular PP of a verb they may never have learned. *Taken together, however, all the forms of αἱρέω* (simple form plus all the compound forms built on it) *occur 62x, and the 3rd PP alone occurs 40x.* By the standards of most first-year courses, a word that occurs that often ought to have been learned as part of the basic introduction to Greek!

---

1. Bruce M. Metzger, *Lexical Aids for Students of New Testament Greek*, 3rd ed. (Grand Rapids: Baker Academic, 1998).

2. See below on the source for our statistics.

3. For an overview explanation of principal parts (PPs), consult the introduction to Part I, below.

It is imperative, therefore, that while students read and memorize lexical stems, *they must also be drilling on the most commonly occurring irregular stems*.

Of course, any good first-year NT Greek primer lays a foundation of vocabulary and lists the PPs of most of its verbs. In all vocabulary acquisition, however, regular cycles of review are essential. The present list collects all the stems that will have been studied in the first semesters of work, sifts out the least frequent, adds others, and arranges them from more to less common. For instance, in the first year of study one learns φέρω (I bear, carry) and its different PP stems including the 2ⁿᵈ and 3ʳᵈ. Now, φέρω occurs 192x in all of its forms (simplex + compounds). But of all those, it occurs only 3x as 2ⁿᵈ PP οἴσω. Πίνω occurs 81x in all its forms; its 2ⁿᵈ PP, πίομαι, occurs 4x. Ἐσθίω occurs 177x in all its forms; its 2ⁿᵈ PP, φάγομαι, occurs 5x. There are good pedagogical reasons to utilize the various stems to illustrate the principle of learning PPs for first-year students, but beyond that, for functional purposes, it does not make sense to spend one's time learning a form that occurs only 3–5x in the NT before learning other stems (such as the 3ʳᵈ PP of αἱρέω) that occur far more often. It would make no more sense to do that than it would to prioritize lexical stems that occur only a handful of times over far more common lexemes.

On the principle that irregular or difficult PP stems are to be learned as separate vocabulary items, and on the principle that it is logical to list stems from most frequently to least frequently occurring, a *complement* to the standard lexical stem lists is much needed.[4] That is the intention of this resource.

The goal is that, as students read, say, Matthew 5:29, εἰ δὲ ὁ ὀφθαλμός σου ὁ δεξιὸς σκανδαλίζει σε, ἔξελε αὐτὸν καὶ βάλε ἀπὸ σοῦ, they will more readily identify ἔξελε as the 3ʳᵈ PP of ἐξαιρέω (ἐκ + αἱρέω).

Rather than treating these hard cases as left-overs after all the grammar and vocabulary have been learned, we will place them front and center as a relatively short list that can be mastered with ease. Once a NT text like Matthew 5:29 has been read, there are further challenges for understanding and life. But it must be read.

---

4   For the sake of those who define things carefully, the word "stem" refers to the word form without the augment or ending: λυσα or λαβ. "Principal parts" are the 1/s indic of the tense-systems occurring in it: ἔλυσα or ἔλαβον. Though we operate with these definitions, our effort to direct attention to the *stem* and to encourage students to think in terms of *principal parts* as systems means that we will say things like "the stems listed in Part I," when Part I is in fact a list of inflected forms. It is to be understood that we are directing attention to the various stems *as represented in* the forms listed.

The present list of difficult and irregular Greek verb PPs is designed for students who already have a knowledge of the Greek language that enables them to parse verbal forms and translate at least the easier passages of NT Greek. We have resisted the temptation to reteach those things. Ideally, these students will have begun extending their vocabulary beyond the usual range of beginning grammar textbooks. If their ambition is not merely to translate isolated portions of Greek when necessary but to establish the habit of regular reading, the value of the following list will need little explanation.

The logic behind this list of PPs is simple. Difficult PP stems ought to receive separate attention in vocabulary acquisition, and it is efficient to study stems in descending order of frequency of occurrence. The way to learn irregular and difficult stems is by associating them with their lexical forms and noting their PP number. Given a beginning level study of Greek, including a grasp of the common vocabulary stock, this is all that is necessary to complete the parsing of a difficult or irregular stem and proceed to translation. The frequency of a stem includes all the compound forms built on that stem. If one can recognize the stem, one can parse any of its compound forms. This also means that, even if the separate compound forms occur infrequently, the total number of occurrences of a given stem can be relatively high.

The list was compiled primarily by searching Accordance[1] and *Thesaurus Linguae Graecae*[2] and checking our results against other published lists of stems. We have taken care to ensure that there is accuracy in both stem identification and frequency. At some points there are debated forms, and for some verbs there are alternative stems. *We invite all corrections.* The frequencies given for each stem, even if found to be imprecise here or there, will be close enough to achieve the instructional aim of this list.

This is not intended as a reference work; it is not a database for morphological analysis. It is a learning aid to be used as a step when

---

1. Accordance 11.1.0 © 2015 OakTree Software, based on the NA[27] edition of the Greek NT (see abbreviations). Our frequency blocks serve as well for NA[28]. Our statistics sometimes do not reflect those of Accordance, on which we were dependent for all frequencies. In some cases it is because of our grouping of compound forms, which will be indicated in Part II. Occasionally we disagree with this software's parsing.
2. *Thesaurus Linguae Graecae* [TLG], A Digital Library of Greek Literature. Searched online: http://stephanus.tlg.uci.edu.

moving from beginning language instruction to reading competency. Therefore, we have stripped out anything that would distract from this instructional aim.

The glosses used in Part I are explained in the introduction to that section; we are not attempting an analysis of semantics, but we are offering an aid to the recognition of forms. The lowest frequency block in Part I is 10x, in parallel with Metzger's *Lexical Aids* volume; somewhere below 10x the work of memorization will not receive reinforcement in reading because the form is too rare.[3]

Note the comment in the Preface about how this work intends the phrase "difficult and irregular" in describing these forms. Initially we cast a broad net over 2nd–6th PP stems that a beginning student with that perspective would not intuitively recognize. We have attempted to err on the side of inclusiveness. For example, even though the stems of athematic (-μι) verbs are highly regular, they often fall toward the end of the first year of study and so are less familiar; therefore, we have included the common ones. We include some other verbs that are regular but conceivably present their own challenges (e.g., δέω, which is a short word that occurs primarily as aorist or perfect). Here, too, we welcome input.

But is this approach of plucking out stems and treating them like self-standing entries to be learned in order of frequency a sensible approach? Should we not come at this through morphological patterns so that it is easier to assimilate and retain the information and to reduce the perception of randomness? Yes! In some measure we are assuming a knowledge of the basic and most widespread patterns, which is precisely why most stems that occur in the NT need not be listed here. Beyond that introductory knowledge there already are sufficient aids for developmental or systemic perspectives, the use of which we only encourage.[4] The present resource is merely another approach, perhaps in its own way a little closer to the way native language users pick up these stems. Again, this is a stepping stone toward reading, not a study in morphological systems.

---

3.   Sakae Kubo, *A Reader's Greek–English Lexicon of the New Testament*, Zondervan Greek Reference Series (Grand Rapids: Zondervan, 2015), begins each NT book with a list of "special vocabulary," lexical forms of words that occur less than 50x but more than 5x in the book in question. The ambitious student can do the same for the difficult PP stems of verbs in individual NT books.

4.   One book-length attempt is that of William D. Mounce, *The Morphology of Biblical Greek* (Grand Rapids: Zondervan, 1994). On a more limited scale but with great wisdom, Metzger's *Lexical Aids* volume includes helps of this nature. Another work to mention is J. Harold Greenlee, *A New Testament Greek Morpheme Lexicon* (Grand Rapids: Zondervan, 1983). From the broader perspective of these works, there is far less "irregularity" in the morphology of the Greek verbal system than might be felt when it is first encountered and so, if the system is mastered, "difficulty" is much reduced. We strongly encourage students to pursue this level of understanding and expect that the practice of regular reading will assist toward that end.

Part I of this Handy Guide gets to the nub in listing the PPs of the simplex stems, but for almost all of these words the counts are cumulative counts of word groups. Some of the stems never occur in the simplex form, but only as a compound. Both for instructors who wish to gain a sense of the range of the groups and the basis of the counts, and for students who wish to see the actual words that are represented by the forms of Part I, Part II is vital. Moreover, by listing the verbs in Part II in order of descending frequency, with the counts, students can proceed from the vocabulary work of Part I to that of Part II in the effort to establish their mastery of these verbs. The contents of Part II have been reduced to what is completely essential and appropriate to the stated aims of the book. For instance, statistics that shaped Part I as well as details about forms that would only distract from the task at hand are not included.

SPECIAL NOTES:

No single lens could provide optimal exposure to all stems. By their very nature the stems we are listing resist simplification—and simplification was our goal. Because of the frequency of aorist forms in general and unaugmented aorist forms in particular, we began by using infinitives as the default for all forms. This was not the best lens for the future and perfect, however. We therefore have chosen to use 1/s indicative forms as the default, as is usual, but for aorist forms to add the infinitive in brackets. Students composing vocabulary cards from this list may prefer to use the unaugmented forms for drilling.

Verbs that appear only in middle form in the NT will be listed with middle endings. Those stems that occur only in compound forms are preceded by a hyphen.

The correlation of PPs with tenses and voices in our lists will follow conventional systems with the understanding that the 6th PP contains verbs that are middle (so-called "deponent" verbs, among others), as soundly highlighted in recent discussions.[5] Arguably, its full scope falls within the domain of the middle voice; the passive is one rendering. As always, morphological tags mask underlying semantic complexities, which will be learned by advancing students. In the same spirit, we have retained the labels "present," "aorist," etc. Instructors and students who prefer other parsing labels need only pencil them into the chart in the Preliminary Notes of Part I.

---

5.   See Rachel Aubrey, "Motivated Categories, Middle Voice, and Passive Morphology," in *The Greek Verb Revisited: A Fresh Approach for Biblical Exegesis*, ed. Steven E. Runge and Christopher J. Fresch (Bellingham, WA: Lexham Press, 2016), 563–625. More accessible is Constantine R. Campbell, "Deponency and the Middle Voice," in his *Advances in the Study of Greek: New Insights for Reading the New Testament* (Grand Rapids: Zondervan, 2015), 91–104. .

In a few cases it has made sense to list separately an imperfect tense form (e.g., εἶχον) or an aorist in infinitive or participle form (e.g., ἰδεῖν) due to its distinctive appearance. The separate listings of the infinitive or participle occur in the same frequency block as their indicative forms. Such forms are always parsed in addition to giving the PP number.

Athematic (-μι) verbs present a special challenge since some use a 1st aorist stem for the aorist active indicative and the 2nd aorist stem for everything else built in the 3rd PP system. Where this is the case we list the 1st aorist as an indicative form in its own frequency block (e.g., ἔθηκα); this includes the 1st aorist of ἵστημι. The 2nd aorists of all -μι verbs are listed using the genitive singular participle form according to the frequency of occurrence of that stem (e.g., δόντος, βάντος).[6]

The verb εἶμι (I go), occurs 7x as a present participle, 3x as a present infinitive, 3x as imperfect, and 1x as present indicative. We group these under one count (14x) and give the full paradigm at the end.

The frequency categorization of 4th PP and 5th PP stems includes both perfect and pluperfect forms. In a couple of places we listed a pluperfect form separately in the same frequency block (e.g., εἱστήκειν) due to its distinctive appearance and frequency of occurrence.

The verb οἶδα is a special case. The 4th PP is the lexical form and is well known from beginning grammars, but the εἰδ- stem (used for the subjunctive, imperative, participle, infinitive, and pluperfect) is probably overlooked, as is the pluperfect, ᾔδειν.[7] We have listed the εἰδ- forms together in the same frequency block (represented by the infinitive, εἰδέναι, and the pluperfect indicative), though the pluperfect on its own is less common.

Some verbs (e.g., ἀνοίγω) have more than one form of a PP stem. We have listed the most common one and added the others in parentheses at the same point.

A few verbs have 1st and 2nd aorist 6th PP stems (e.g., ἀνοίγω, τάσσω). We have listed such forms separately in the same frequency block.

A few out-of-the-way forms of γίνομαι and εἰμί are supplied because they occur above the threshold of 10x, yet so seldom that they may have been overlooked or forgotten by beginning students. The frequency for the form ἔσομαι represents all future forms of εἰμί. The frequency for the imperative or optative forms of γίνομαι or εἰμί represents the particular inflection listed (e.g., γίνομαι occurs 17x as 3/s aor mid opt γένοιτο); likewise the infinitive εἶναι.

---

6. The genitive participle is used for the 2nd aorist 3rd PP of -μι verbs because for δίδωμι, τίθημι, and ἵημι the aorist active indicative does not form on that stem and because the infinitive involves a lengthening that obscures the stem. For ἵστημι, -βαίνω, and γινώσκω, which do form the aorist active indicative on the 2nd aorist 3rd PP stem (all three are athematic in the 3rd PP), we give both that form (aorist active indicative) and the genitive participle in the same frequency block. Following all of these participle entries we supply the infinitive as well in brackets.

7. In fact εἶδον (serves as 3rd PP of ὁράω) and οἶδα have the same root.

LIST OF SIGLA
AND ABBREVIATIONS

-	A hyphen preceding a verbal form (-ἔβην) indicates that it occurs only in a compound form in the NT.
( )	Parentheses indicate alternative verbal forms in Part I. In Part II these indicate forms that do not occur in the NT.
(ABCDEFGHIJ)	Superscripted letters in parentheses refer to frequency blocks in Part I. See Part II, preliminary notes.
[ ]	A form in square brackets is the infinitive form of the verb in either the 3rd or 6th principal part.
{	A curly bracket introduces a gloss or a cross reference to another verb form.
1, 2, 3, 4, 5, 6	Arabic numbers refer to particular principal part stems of the verb. In parsing, these are constructed with a slash (/) and pertain to the person number of the verb (e.g. 1/s = first person singular).
act	active
aor	aorist
BDAG	Walter Bauer, Frederick Danker, W. F. Arndt, and F. W. Gingrich, *A Greek–English Lexicon of the New Testament and Other Early Christian Literature*, 3rd ed. (Chicago: University of Chicago Press, 2000).
cf.	compare (*confer*)
e.g.	for example (*exempli gratia*)
etc.	and the rest (*et cetera*)
fut	future
gen	genitive
imperf	imperfect
impv	imperative
indic	indicative
infin	infinitive
intrans	intransitive
LXX	Septuagint
mid	middle
NA27	Kurt Aland et al., *Novum Testamentum Graece*. 27th edition. Stuttgart: Deutsche Bibelgesellschaft, 1993.
NT	New Testament
opt	optative

partic	participle
pass	passive
perf	perfect
pl	plural
pluperf	pluperfect
PP	Principal Part. See the explanation for principal parts in Part I, Preliminary Notes (page 21). "PP stem" is shorthand for, "the stem of the Principal Part."
PPs	Principal Parts (plural)
pres	present
s	singular
subj	subjunctive
trans	transitive

FREQUENCY LIST OF DIFFICULT AND IRREGULAR PRINCIPAL PARTS

PRELIMINARY NOTES

The following list is structured in blocks of frequency, as in standard lists of lexical forms. It includes all lemmas (the simple stem vs. the compounds) of those that occur 10x or more. This list will not give a separate entry for all of the compound forms of, say, ἄγω (such as, συνάγω), but only for the simple stem. The principle is that only the simple stem need be drilled since the compounds all follow suit. The counts represent all the occurrences of the stem in question, both simplex and compounds.

As for principal parts, the following is taken as known:

1st PP = present and imperfect (all voices)
2nd PP = future active and middle
3rd PP = aorist active and middle
4th PP = perfect and pluperfect active
5th PP = perfect and pluperfect middle and passive
6th PP = aorist and future passive

The forms will be 1/s indicative as a rule; exceptions are noted. If it is an aorist (augmented) form, we give the infinitive in brackets so that the unaugmented stem can be seen. The 2nd *aorist stems of -μι verbs are represented by genitive singular participles* with the infinitive in brackets; if the 2nd aorist stem of a -μι verb is used for the aorist active indicative we also show that form in the same frequency block as the participle form. Further explanations are given above under the "Note to Instructors and Interested Students."

The lexical form in the parsing of each verb is not glossed because in most cases it represents a group of verbs that share a stem (see Part II); in the case of some verbs only compound forms, not the simplex, appear in the NT. For the sake of reference, however, we have given a simplified gloss of the listed form to the right.[1] The gloss does not represent the tense or mood of the verb form in question. It is simply a common gloss associated with the lexical form of the simple stem. If the stem appears only in compound forms, for the sake of the gloss we employ the most common compound for the PP listed.

Here are two sample entries from Block F, forms that occur 29–25x:

ἐβλήθην [βληθῆναι] 6 βάλλω   {throw
εἴρηκα 4 λέγω   {say

In the first example, ἐβλήθην—a PP of the verb βάλλω and all its compounds together—occurs within the range of 29–25x. The infinitive (unaugmented) form is βληθῆναι. The form ἐβλήθην is the 6th PP of βάλλω. In the second example, εἴρηκα is the 4th PP of the verb λέγω. It is assumed that the student knows what is built on these PP stems and the regular conjugation of the tenses.

The following example is from Block G (forms occurring 24–20x in the NT):

ἠνοίχθην (or ἀνεῴχθην/ἠνεῴχθην) [ἀνοιχθῆναι] 6 ἀνοίγω   {open

Almost everything works the same: ἠνοίχθην is the 6th PP of ἀνοίγω, and its unaugmented infinitive is provided in square brackets. The exception in this entry is that alternative forms of the same PP are added in parentheses.

Finally, the following example is from Block B (forms occurring 199-100x in the NT):

-βάντος 3 gen partic -βαίνω [-βῆναι]   {see -ἔβην

A genitive participle is used to represent the 2nd aorist of all of the -μι verbs in our list, including those like -βαίνω that do form the indicative active on that stem. Thus -βάντος (hyphenated because it occurs only in compound forms) represents the 3rd PP of -βαίνω. Following the parsing we supply the infinitive in brackets. When the gloss to the right says "see -ἔβην" (or something like it), it is always a reference to another entry for the related stem (far left) within the same frequency block. Thus, within the same block we find this entry:

-ἔβην [-βῆναι] 3 -βαίνω   {ἀναβαίνω, go up

Because this stem appears only in compounds (as indicated by the hyphen), to the right the most common compound is used to illustrate a gloss.

---

1.   Glosses come from BDAG.

DIFFICULT AND IRREGULAR FORMS OCCURRING 10X OR MORE IN THE NEW TESTAMENT

A. FORMS OCCURRING 1000–200X IN THE NT

δόντος 3 gen partic δίδωμι [δοῦναι] {give
ἐγενόμην [γενέσθαι] 3 γίνομαι {become
ἔδωκα 3 δίδωμι {give
εἶδον (or εἶδα) [ἰδεῖν] 3 ὁράω {see
εἶπον (or εἶπα) [εἰπεῖν] 3 λέγω {say
ἐκρίθην [κριθῆναι] 6 κρίνω {judge
ἔλαβον [λαβεῖν] 3 λαμβάνω {take
ἔστην [στῆναι] 3 ἵστημι {stand
ἦλθον (or ἦλθα) [ἐλθεῖν] 3 ἔρχομαι {come, go
ἰδεῖν 3 aor act infin ὁράω {see εἶδον
στάντος 3 gen partic ἵστημι [στῆναι] {see ἔστην

B. FORMS OCCURRING 199–100X IN THE NT

-βάντος 3 gen partic -βαίνω [-βῆναι] {see -ἔβην
γνόντος 3 gen partic γινώσκω [γνῶναι] {see ἔγνων
ἔβαλον [βαλεῖν] 3 βάλλω {throw
-ἔβην [-βῆναι] 3 -βαίνω {ἀναβαίνω, go up
ἔγνων [γνῶναι] 3 γινώσκω {know
εἰδέναι 4 perf act infin οἶδα {know
εἶναι pres infin εἰμί {be, exist
εἱστήκειν 4 pluperf act indic ἵστημι {see ἔστηκα
ἔπεσον (or ἔπεσα) [πεσεῖν] 3 πίπτω {fall
ἔσομαι future εἰμί {see εἶναι
-ἔστειλα [-στεῖλαι] 3 στέλλω {ἀποστέλλω, send
ἔστηκα (gen partic ἐστηκότος, ἑστῶτος) 4 ἵστημι {stand
ἤγαγον [ἀγαγεῖν] 3 ἄγω {lead
ᾔδειν 4 pluperf act indic οἶδα {see εἰδέναι

C. FORMS OCCURRING 99–60X IN THE NT

γέγονα 4 γίνομαι {become
δώσω 2 δίδωμι {give
ἐδόθην [δοθῆναι] 6 δίδωμι {give
-ἔθανεν [-θανεῖν] 3 θνήσκω {ἀποθνήσκω, die
εἶχον imperf act indic ἔχω {have
-ἕντος 3 gen partic -ἥμι [-εἶναι] {ἀφίημι, let go
εὗρον [εὑρεῖν] 3 εὑρίσκω {find
ἔφαγον [φαγεῖν] 3 ἐσθίω {eat
-ἤγγειλα [-ἀγγεῖλαι] 3 ἀγγέλλω {ἀπαγγέλλω, report
ἤνεγκα [ἐνέγκαι] 3 φέρω {carry
ἦρα [ἆραι] 3 αἴρω {lift up
θέντος 3 gen partic τίθημι [θεῖναι] {lay, put

D. Forms occurring 59–40x in the NT

ἐγενήθην [γενηθῆναι] 6 γίνομαι	{become
ἔθηκα 3 τίθημι	{lay, put
-εἶλον (or -εἶλα) [-ἐλεῖν] 3 αἱρέω	{ἀναιρέω, take away
ἐκλήθην [κληθῆναι] 6 καλέω	{call
ἔκρινα [κρῖναι] 3 κρίνω	{judge
-ἔκτεινα [-κτεῖναι] 3 -κτείνω	{ἀποκτείνω, kill
ἐλεύσομαι 2 ἔρχομαι	{come, go
ἐλήλυθα 4 ἔρχομαι	{come, go
ἔμεινα [μεῖναι] 3 μένω	{remain
ἐρῶ 2 λέγω	{say
ἔφη imperf act indic 3/s φημί	{say
ἠγέρθην [ἐγερθῆναι] 6 ἐγείρω	{wake, get up
ἤνοιξα (or ἀνέῳξα/ἠνέῳξα) [ἀνοῖξαι] 3 ἀνοίγω	{open
ἤχθην [ἀχθῆναι] 6 ἄγω	{lead
-ὤλεσα [-ὀλέσαι] 3 -ὄλλυμι	{ἀπόλλυμι, ruin

E. Forms occurring 39–30x in the NT

δέδωκα 4 δίδωμι	{give
ἔδειξα [δεῖξαι] 3 δείκνυμι	{point out, show
ἔπιον [πιεῖν] 3 πίνω	{drink
ἐστάθην [σταθῆναι] 6 ἵστημι	{stand
ἔταξα [τάξαι] 3 τάσσω	{arrange
ἑώρακα 4 ὁράω	{see
ἤγειρα [ἐγεῖραι] 3 ἐγείρω	{wake, get up
-ἧκα 3 -ἵημι	{ἀφίημι, let go
ἧψα [ἅψαι] 3 ἅπτω	{light, kindle
ὄψομαι 2 ὁράω	{see
στήσω 2 ἵστημι	{set, place

F. Forms occurring 29–25x in the NT

δέδεμαι 5 δέω	{bind
ἐβλήθην [βληθῆναι] 6 βάλλω	{throw
εἴρηκα 4 λέγω	{say
-ἔλεξα [-λέξαι] 3 λέγω	{ἐκλέγομαι, choose
-ἔλιπον [-λιπεῖν] 3 λείπω	{καταλείπω, leave behind
ἔπαθον [παθεῖν] 3 πάσχω	{experience, suffer
ἐρρέθην [ῥηθῆναι] 6 λέγω	{say
ἐστράφην [στραφῆναι] 6 στρέφω	{pass: turn around
ἔσχον [σχεῖν] 3 ἔχω	{have
εὑρέθην [εὑρεθῆναι] 6 εὑρίσκω	{find
ἔφυγον [φυγεῖν] 3 φεύγω	{flee
-ἤντησα [-ἀντῆσαι] 3 -ἀντάω	{καταντάω, come, arrive
ῥηθῆναι 6 aor pass infin λέγω	{see ἐρρέθην
ὤφθην [ὀφθῆναι] 6 ὁράω	{see

G. Forms occurring 24–20X in the NT

ἔγνωκα 4 γινώσκω	{know
ἔδησα [δῆσαι] 3 δέω	{bind
ἕξω 2 ἔχω	{have
ἐπλήσθην [πλησθῆναι] 6 πίμπλημι	{fill, fulfill
ἔστησα 3 ἵστημι	{set, place
ἐτέθην [τεθῆναι] 6 τίθημι	{lay, put
εὑρήσω 2 εὑρίσκω	{find
ἐχάρην [χαρῆναι] 6 χαίρω	{pass: rejoice
ἡμάρτησα [ἁμαρτῆσαι] 3 ἁμαρτάνω	{sin
ἥμαρτον [ἁμαρτεῖν] 3 ἁμαρτάνω	{see ἡμάρτησα
ἠνοίγην [ἀνοιγῆναι] 6 ἀνοίγω	{see ἠνοίχθην
ἠνοίχθην (or ἀνεῴχθην/ἠνεῴχθην) [ἀνοιχθῆναι] 6 ἀνοίγω	{open
λήμψομαι 2 λαμβάνω	{take
μνήσθην [μνησθῆναι] 6 μιμνήσκω	{μιμνήσκομαι, remember
ὤμοσα [ὀμόσαι or ὀμνύναι] 3 ὀμνύω	{swear

H. Forms occurring 19–15X in the NT

βέβλημαι 5 βάλλω	{throw
γένοιτο 3 aor mid opt γίνομαι	{become
γνώσομαι 2 γινώσκω	{know
ἔδραμον [δραμεῖν] 3 τρέχω	{run
-έθην [-εθῆναι] 6 -ίημι	{ἀφίημι, let go
ἐκέρδανα [κερδᾶναι/κερδῆναι] 3 κερδαίνω	{gain
ἐκέρδησα [κερδῆσαι] 3 κερδαίνω	{gain
ἐκήρυξα [κηρύξαι] 3 κηρύσσω	{announce
ἔκοψα [κόψαι] 3 κόπτω	{cut off
ἔμαθον [μαθεῖν] 3 μανθάνω	{learn
-ἐτειλάμην [-τείλασθαι] 3 -τέλλω	{ἐντέλλω, pass: command
ἐτέλεσα [τελέσαι] 3 τελέω	{bring to an end, accomplish
ἔτυχον [τυχεῖν] 3 τυγχάνω	{meet, attain
ἤρθην [ἀρθῆναι] 6 αἴρω	{lift up
κέκλημαι 5 καλέω	{call
κρινῶ 2 κρίνω	{judge
-ὀλέσω 2 -ὄλλυμι	{ἀπόλλυμι, ruin
-ὀλῶ 2 -ὄλλυμι	{see -ὀλέσω
πέποιθα 4 πείθω	{convince; perf: trust, rely on

I. Forms occurring 14–13X in the NT

-βέβηκα 4 -βαίνω	{ἀναβαίνω, go up
δέδομαι 5 δίδωμι	{give
ἐγνώσθην [γνωσθῆναι] 6 γινώσκω	{know
ἔδοξα [δόξαι] 3 δοκέω	{think, believe
-ἐκαλύφθην [-καλυφθῆναι] 6 καλύπτω	{ἀποκαλύπτω, reveal
-ἐκτάνθην [-κτανθῆναι] 6 -κτείνω	{ἀποκτείνω, kill

ἔνιψα [νίψαι] 3 νίπτω — {wash
ἔσπειρα [σπεῖραι] 3 σπείρω — {sow seed
ἔστω (ἤτω 2x) pres impv 3/s εἰμί — {be, exist
-ἔτεινα [-τεῖναι] 3 -τείνω — {ἐκτείνω, stretch out
ἐφάνην [φανῆναι] 6 φαίνω — {pass: shine, appear
ἐφύλαξα [φυλάξαι] 3 φυλάσσω — {watch, protect
-ἔχεα [-χέαι] 3 -χέω — {ἐκχέω, pour out
-ἰέναι pres act infin -εἶμι — {ἔπειμι, come upon
-ἰόντος pres gen partic -εἶμι — {see -ἰέναι

ἀκήκοα 4 ἀκούω — {hear
ἀνέῳγμαι (or ἠνέῳγμαι) 5 ἀνοίγω — {open
γενήσομαι 2 γίνομαι — {become
δείξω 2 δείκνυμι — {point out, show
ἐγήγερμαι 5 ἐγείρω — {wake, get up
εἴη pres opt 3/s εἰμί — {be, exist
ἔκυψα [κύψαι] 3 κύπτω — {bend down
-ἐλήμφθην [-λημφθῆναι] 6 λαμβάνω — {ἀναλαμβάνω, take up
ἐξηράνθην [ξηρανθῆναι] 6 ξηραίνω — {dry, dry up
-ἔπλευσα [-πλεῦσαι] 3 πλέω — {sail, ἀποπλέω, sail away
ἔπραξα [πρᾶξαι] 3 πράσσω — {do, accomplish
ἐσπάρην [σπαρῆναι] 6 σπείρω — {sow
-ἔσταλκα 4 στέλλω — {ἀποστέλλω, send away
-ἔσταλμαι 5 στέλλω — {ἀποστέλλω, send away
-ἐτάγην [-ταγῆναι] 6 τάσσω — {see -ἐτάχθην
-ἐτάχθην [-ταχθῆναι] 6 τάσσω — {ὑποτάσσω, subordinate
ἐτελέσθην [τελεσθῆναι] 6 τελέω — {bring to an end, accomplish
-ἐτράπην [-τραπῆναι] 6 -τρέπω — {ἐντρέπω, pass: have regard for
ἠδυνήθην [δυνηθῆναι] 6 δύναμαι — {am able
ἠνέχθην [ἐνεχθῆναι] 6 φέρω — {carry
ἤνοιγμαι (or ἀνέῳγμαι/ἠνέῳγμαι) 5 ἀνοίγω — {open
θήσω 2 τίθημι — {lay, put
-κτενῶ 2 -κτείνω — {ἀποκτείνω, kill
τέταγμαι 5 τάσσω — {arrange, put in place

PART II

ALPHABETICAL LIST OF VERBS
WITH THEIR COMPOUNDS

PRELIMINARY NOTES

All the verbs represented in the above list in order of frequency are listed alphabetically below. Three things will be supplied for each. First, *all* the PPs of that verb will be listed, just as in any dictionary except that we give both the indicative and an infinitive or participle form for the PP stems featured in the frequency list; these forms from Part I are bolded. Many PPs that are not bolded occur frequently in the NT but are excluded from our frequency list since they should be readily recognizable given any standard introduction to the grammar and vocabulary of the NT. Forms that do not occur in the NT are placed in parentheses. Second, the superscript letter following each bolded entry (e.g., **-ἤγγειλα, -ἀγγεῖλαι**[C]) indicates in which frequency block that stem is included in Part I. Third, all the NT's compound forms of each verb are listed underneath it in descending order of frequency (the number after each is the full count for that verb in the NT) and with *simplified* glosses.[1] In this way it will be apparent how broadly that verb occurs in the NT in all its forms. It might also be another way for students to expand their vocabulary as they observe the patterns of meanings among the compounds.

Though the list of forms in Part I stops at those that occur 10x or more, in the following we list *all* of the compounds for each lemma given, including compound forms that occur only once or twice in the NT.

---

1. Glosses come from BDAG (see preliminary comments to part I). A comma indicates a synonymous gloss within categories and a semi-colon indicates a second, third, or fourth listed meaning in BDAG.

ALPHABETICAL LIST OF VERBS WITH PRINCIPAL PARTS AND COMPOUNDS

ἀγγέλλω

1 ἀγγέλλω
2 -ἀγγελῶ
3 **-ἤγγειλα, -ἀγγεῖλαι** [C]

4 (-ἤγγελκα)
5 -ἤγγελμαι
6 (-ἠγγέλθην) or -ἠγγέλην

Ἀγγέλλω and compounds that share its principal parts:

ἀπαγγέλλω	report (back), proclaim	45
παραγγέλλω	give orders, command	32
καταγγέλλω	proclaim, announce	18
ἐπαγγέλλομαι	promise, profess	15
ἀναγγέλλω	report, disclose	14
διαγγέλλω	proclaim, spread the news	3
ἐξαγγέλλω	proclaim, report	2
προεπαγγέλλω	promise before(hand)	2
προκαταγγέλλω	foretell	2
ἀγγέλλω	announce	1

ἄγω

1 ἄγω
2 ἄξω
3 ἦξα, ἄξαι
  ἤγαγον, ἀγαγεῖν [B]

4 (ἦχα)
5 -ἦγμαι
6 **ἤχθην, ἀχθῆναι** [D]

Ἄγω and compounds that share its principal parts:

ὑπάγω	go away; go; die	79
ἄγω	lead, bring	67
συνάγω	gather; reconcile	59
ἀνάγω	lead up; mid/pass put out to sea	23
προάγω	lead forward, go before	20
ἀπάγω	lead off	15
ἐξάγω	lead out	12
εἰσάγω	bring/lead in	11
παράγω	go away; introduce; pass away	10
κατάγω	lead/bring down	9
ἐπισυνάγω	gather together	8

περιάγω	lead around	6
προσάγω	bring, come near	4
ἐπάγω	bring on (usu. something bad)	3
ἐπανάγω	go out; return	3
συναπάγω	lead away with; accommodate	3
διάγω	live	2
μετάγω	guide, move	2
παρεισάγω	bring, introduce	1

αἱρέω

1 αἱρῶ   4 (-ᾕρηκα)
2 αἱρήσω or -ἑλῶ   5 -ᾕρημαι
3 -εἷλον (or -εἷλα), -ἑλεῖν (D)   6 -ᾑρέθην

Αἱρέω and compounds that share its principal parts:

ἀναιρέω	take away; destroy	24
ἀφαιρέω	take away, remove	10
καθαιρέω	take down; destroy	9
ἐξαιρέω	take out; set free	8
περιαιρέω	take away	5
αἱρέω	take; mid: choose	3
διαιρέω	distribute, divide	2
προαιρέω	bring/take out; choose (for oneself)	1

αἴρω

1 αἴρω   4 ἦρκα
2 ἀρῶ   5 ἦρμαι
3 ἦρα, ἆραι (C)   6 ἤρθην, ἀρθῆναι (H)

Αἴρω and compounds that share its principal parts:

αἴρω	lift up; take away	101
ἐπαίρω	lift up; be in opposition	19
ἀπαίρω	take away; depart	3
συναίρω	settle accounts	3
ὑπεραίρω	rise, exalt oneself	3
μεταίρω	go away	2
ἐξαίρω	remove, drive away	1

ἀκούω

1 ἀκούω	4 ἀκήκοα, ἀκηκοέναι [J]
2 ἀκούσω	5 (ἤκουσμαι)
3 ἤκουσα	6 ἠκούσθην

Ἀκούω and compounds that share its principal parts:

ἀκούω	hear, grant a hearing, learn	428
ὑπακούω	obey; hear; open (door)	21
εἰσακούω	obey, hear	5
παρακούω	overhear; ignore; disobey	3
διακούω	give (someone) a hearing	1
ἐπακούω	hear; heed	1
προακούω	hear beforehand	1

ἁμαρτάνω

1 ἁμαρτάνω	4 ἡμάρτηκα
2 ἁμαρτήσω	5 (ἡμάρτημαι)
3 ἡμάρτησα, ἁμαρτῆσαι	6 ἡμαρτήθην
ἥμαρτον, ἁμαρτεῖν [G]	

Ἁμαρτάνω and compounds that share its principal parts:

ἁμαρτάνω	sin	45
προαμαρτάνω	sin beforehand	2

-ἀντάω

1 -ἀντάω	4 -ήντηκα
2 -ἀντήσω	5 –
3 -ήντησα, -ἀντῆσαι [F]	6 (-ἠντήθην)

Compounds that share the principal parts of -ἀντάω:

καταντάω	come, arrive	13
ὑπαντάω	meet; encounter	10
συναντάω	meet; happen	6
ἀπαντάω	meet (someone)	2

ἀνοίγω

1 ἀνοίγω
2 ἀνοίξω/(ἠνοίξω/ἀνέῳξω)

3 ἤνοιξα/ἀνέῳξα/ἠνέῳξα,
  ἀνοῖξαι (D)

4 ἀνέῳγα
5 ἤνοιγμαι/ἀνέῳγμαι/ἠνέῳγμαι,
  ἠνοῖχθαι/ἀνεῴχθαι/ἠνεῴχθαι (J)
6 ἠνοίχθην/ἀνεῴχθην/ἠνεῴχθην
  or ἠνοίγην, ἀνοιχθῆναι/
  ἀνεῳχθῆναι or ἀνοιγῆναι (G)

Ἀνοίγω and compounds that share its principal parts:

ἀνοίγω	open	77
διανοίγω	open; explain	8

ἅπτω

1 ἅπτω
2 (ἅψω)
3 ἦψα, ἅψαι (E)

4 (ἦφα)
5 (ἧμμαι)
6 -ήφθην

Ἅπτω and compounds that share its principal parts:

ἅπτω	light, kindle; touch	39
ἀνάπτω	kindle	2
καθάπτω	take hold of, seize	1
περιάπτω	kindle	1

-βαίνω

1 -βαίνω
2 -βήσομαι
3 -ἔβην, -βῆναι,
  partic -βάς, -βάντος (B)

4 -βέβηκα, -βεβηκέναι (I)
5 –
6 (-ἐβάθην)

Compounds that share the principal parts of -βαίνω:

ἀναβαίνω	go up, ascend	82
καταβαίνω	come/go/climb down	81
ἐμβαίνω	embark	16
μεταβαίνω	go, pass over; pass: pass on	12

συμβαίνω	go along with; happen	8
ἐπιβαίνω	mount, board; set foot in	6
προβαίνω	go ahead; advance in years	5
ἀποβαίνω	go away; turn out	4
διαβαίνω	go through, cross	3
παραβαίνω	go aside; transgress, break	3
συναναβαίνω	come/go up with	2
ἐκβαίνω	go out, come from	1
προσαναβαίνω	go up, move up	1
συγκαταβαίνω	go down with someone	1
ὑπερβαίνω	go beyond; trespass, sin	1

βάλλω

1 βάλλω	4 βέβληκα	
2 βαλῶ	5 βέβλημαι, βεβλῆσθαι (H)	
3 ἔβαλον or ἔβαλα, βαλεῖν (B)	6 ἐβλήθην, βληθῆναι (F)	

Βάλλω and compounds that share its principal parts:

βάλλω	throw; drive out; put, place	122
ἐκβάλλω	drive out; send out; remove	81
περιβάλλω	lay, put around; put on	23
ἐπιβάλλω	throw over; throw oneself; fall to	18
συμβάλλω	converse; consider; compare	6
ὑπερβάλλω	go beyond, surpass	5
ἀποβάλλω	take off; reject; remove	2
καταβάλλω	throw down; found	2
προβάλλω	put forward; put out	2
ἀμφιβάλλω	cast	1
ἀναβάλλω	mid: adjourn (a trial)	1
ἀντιβάλλω	exchange	1
διαβάλλω	being charges, inform	1
ἐμβάλλω	throw	1
μεταβάλλω	change (thinking)	1
παραβάλλω	throw to; give up; compare	1
παρεμβάλλω	put around; insinuate	1
ὑποβάλλω	instigate, suborn	1

γίνομαι

1 γίνομαι
2 γενήσομαι, γενήσεσθαι [J]
3 ἐγενόμην, γενέσθαι [A]

4 γέγονα, γεγονέναι [C]
5 γεγένημαι
6 ἐγενήθην, γενηθῆναι [D]

Γίνομαι and compounds that share its principal parts:

γίνομαι	become, be born; made; arise; happen	669
παραγίνομαι	draw near; appear; stand by	37
διαγίνομαι	pass/elapse (of time)	3
ἀπογίνομαι	die	1
ἐπιγίνομαι	come to pass	1
προγίνομαι	be born earlier, happen before	1
συμπαραγίνομαι	come together, to the aid of	1

γινώσκω

1 γινώσκω
2 γνώσομαι, γνώσεσθαι [H]
3 ἔγνων, γνῶναι [B]

4 ἔγνωκα, ἐγνωκέναι [G]
5 ἔγνωσμαι
6 ἐγνώσθην, γνωσθῆναι [I]

Γινώσκω and compounds that share its principal parts:

γινώσκω	know; learn (of); understand; perceive	222
ἐπιγινώσκω	know; learn; recognize; acknowledge	44
ἀναγινώσκω	read; read aloud (for public hearing)	32
προγινώσκω	have foreknowledge (of); choose beforehand	5
καταγινώσκω	condemn, convict	3
διαγινώσκω	determine; decide/hear (a case)	2

δείκνυμι

1 δείκνυμι
2 δείξω, δείξειν [J]
3 ἔδειξα, δεῖξαι [E]

4 (δέδειχα)
5 -δέδειγμαι
6 ἐδείχθην

Δείκνυμι and compounds that share its principal parts:

δείκνυμι	point out, show; explain, prove	30

ἐνδείκνυμι	show, demonstrate	11
ἐπιδείκνυμι	show; represent; demonstrate	7
ὑποδείκνυμι	indicate; show, give direction	6
ἀποδείκνυμι	make render; show forth; prove	4
ἀναδείκνυμι	show clearly appoint	2

δέω

1 δέω	4 δέδεκα
2 δήσω	5 δέδεμαι, δεδέσθαι (F)
3 ἔδησα, δῆσαι (G)	6 ἐδέθην

Δέω and compounds that share its principal parts:

δέω	bind, tie	43
ὑποδέω	bind beneath, put on	3
καταδέω	bind up	1
περιδέω	bind up, wrap around	1
συνδέω	bind with; imprison	1

δίδωμι

1 δίδωμι	4 δέδωκα, δεδωκέναι (E)
2 δώσω, δώσειν (C)	5 δέδομαι, δεδόσθαι (I)
3 ἔδωκα (A)	6 ἐδόθην, δοθῆναι (C)
gen partic δόντος, infin δοῦναι (A)	

Δίδωμι and compounds that share its principal parts:

δίδωμι	give, donate; produce	415
παραδίδωμι	hand over; commend; hand down; allow	119
ἀποδίδωμι	give; pay; give back; recompense	48
ἐπιδίδωμι	give; surrender	9
ἀνταποδίδωμι	repay, pay back	7
μεταδίδωμι	give (a part of), impart	5
διαδίδωμι	distribute	4
ἐκδίδωμι	lease	4
ἀναδίδωμι	deliver, hand over	1
προδίδωμι	give in advance; betray	1

δοκέω

1 δοκῶ   4 (δέδοκα)
2 (δόξω)   5 (δέδογμαι)
3 ἔδοξα, δόξαι (I)   6 (ἐδοκήθην)

Δοκέω (think, believe; be recognized as) has no compound forms in the NT.

δύναμαι

1 δύναμαι   4 (δεδύνηκα)
2 δυνήσομαι   5 (δεδύνημαι)
3 (ἠδυνάμην)   6 ἠδυνήθην (or ἐδυνήθην), δυνηθῆναι
                        (or δυνασθῆναι)(J)

Δύναμαι (can, am able) has no compound forms in the NT.

ἐγείρω

1 ἐγείρω   4 (ἐγρήγορα)
2 ἐγερῶ   5 ἐγήγερμαι, ἐγηγέρθαι (J)
3 ἤγειρα, ἐγεῖραι (E) 6 ἠγέρθην, ἐγερθῆναι (D)

Ἐγείρω and compounds that share its principal parts:

ἐγείρω	wake; wake up; get up	144
διεγείρω	wake up, arouse	6
συνεγείρω	awaken with; raise with	3
ἐξεγείρω	awaken; raise (from the dead)	2
ἐπεγείρω	arouse, excite, stir up	2

εἰμί   See appendix for full conjugation

Present εἰμί, εἶναι (B)   Future ἔσομαι, ἔσεσθαι (B)

Εἰμί and compounds that share its principal parts:

εἰμί	be, exist, is	2462

πάρειμι	be present, at one's disposal	24
ἄπειμι	be absent	8
ἔνειμι	be in, it is possible	7
σύνειμι	be with	2
συμπάρειμι	be together, be present	1

-εἶμι   See appendix for full conjugation

Present εἶμι, gen partic -ἰόντος, infin ἰέναι (I)

Compounds that share the principal parts of -εἶμι:

ἔπειμι	come upon, come near	5
εἴσειμι	go in/into	4
ἔξειμι	go out, go away	4
σύνειμι	come together	1

ἔρχομαι

1 ἔρχομαι   4 ἐλήλυθα, ἐληλυθέναι (D)
2 ἐλεύσομαι, ἐλεύσεσθαι   5 –
3 ἦλθον (or ἦλθα), ἐλθεῖν (A)   6 –

Ἔρχομαι and compounds that share its principal parts:

ἔρχομαι	come; go; be brought	632
ἐξέρχομαι	go out, come out; die	218
εἰσέρχομαι	enter; come into something	194
ἀπέρχομαι	go away, depart; go out	117
προσέρχομαι	come/go to, approach	86
διέρχομαι	go; review (in one's mind); penetrate	43
συνέρχομαι	assemble; travel together with; come together	30
παρέρχομαι	go by; pass: pass away	29
κατέρχομαι	come down; arrive, put in	16
ἐπέρχομαι	come, arrive; happen	9
προέρχομαι	go forward; go before	9
ἀνέρχομαι	go up	3
περιέρχομαι	go about; make a circuit	3
ἀντιπαρέρχομαι	pass by on the opposite side	2
ἐπανέρχομαι	return	2
παρεισέρχομαι	slip in, come in	2

| συνεισέρχομαι | enter with, go in(to) with | 2 |
| ἐπεισέρχομαι | come (upon come upon) | 1 |

ἐσθίω

1 ἐσθίω
2 φάγομαι (or ἔδομαι)
3 **ἔφαγον, φαγεῖν** (C)

4 (ἐδήδοκα)
5 (ἐδήδεσμαι)
6 (ἐφάγην)

Ἐσθίω and compounds that share its principal parts:

ἐσθίω	eat, consume	158
κατεσθίω	eat up; devour	14
συνεσθίω	eat with	5

εὑρίσκω

1 εὑρίσκω
2 **εὑρήσω, εὑρήσειν** (G)
3 **εὗρον, εὑρεῖν** (C)

4 εὕρηκα
5 (εὕρημαι)
6 **εὑρέθην, εὑρεθῆναι** (F)

Εὑρίσκω and compounds that share its principal parts:

| εὑρίσκω | find; come upon; discover | 149 |
| ἀνευρίσκω | look/search for | 2 |

ἔχω

1 ἔχω imperf **εἶχον** (C)
2 **ἕξω, ἕξειν** (G)
3 **ἔσχον, σχεῖν** (F)

4 ἔσχηκα
5 (-ἔσχημαι)
6 (-ἐσχέθην)

Ἔχω and compounds that share its principal parts:

ἔχω	have, own; have; hold to	708
προσέχω	be concerned about; pay attention to; occupy oneself with	24
ἀπέχω	be paid in full; suffice; be distant	19

κατέχω	prevent, hinder; hold fast; possess	17
παρέχω	give up, offer; grant; cause, make happen	16
ἀνέχω	endure, bear with; accept a complaint	15
συνέχω	hold together; stop; seize, attack	12
μετέχω	share; eat, drink, enjoy	8
ἐπέχω	hold fast; aim at, stop, stay	5
ὑπερέχω	rise above; have power over	5
ἀντέχω	cling to; help (someone)	4
ἐνέχω	bear ill will; be subject to	3
περιέχω	surround; seize; contain	2
προέχω	jut out, excel; have an advantage	1
ὑπέχω	undergo punishment	1

θνήσκω

1 -θνήσκω	4 τέθνηκα
2 -θανοῦμαι	5 –
3 -ἔθανεν, -θανεῖν (C)	6 –

θνήσκω and compounds that share its principal parts:

ἀποθνήσκω	die; face death	111
θνήσκω	die	9
συναποθνήσκω	die with	3

-ἵημι   See appendix for full conjugation

1 -ἵημι	4 (-εἷκα)
2 -ἥσω	5 -εἷμαι
3 -ἧκα (E)	6 -ἕθην, -ἑθῆναι (H)
gen partic -ἕντος, infin -εἷναι (C)	

Compounds that share the principal parts of -ἵημι:

ἀφίημι	let go, send away; cancel; leave	143
συνίημι	understand	26
ἀνίημι	loosen; abandon; give up	4
καθίημι	let down	4
παρίημι	neglect; let fall at the side; careless	2

ἵστημι

1 ἵστημι

2 στήσω, στήσειν (E)

3 ἔστησα (G)
  ἔστην, gen partic στάντος,
  infin στῆναι (A)

4 ἔστηκα, gen partic ἑστηκότος,
  ἑστῶτος (B)

5 (ἔσταμαι)

6 ἐστάθην, σταθῆναι (E)

Ἵστημι and compounds that share its principal parts:

ἵστημι	set, place; put forward; establish; uphold	154
ἀνίστημι	raise; raise up; stand up; come back from the dead	108
παρίστημι	place beside, present, make, offer; be present	41
ἐφίστημι	stand at/near; happen to, overtake	21
καθίστημι	bring, take; appoint; cause	21
ἐξίστημι	confuse; lose one's mind; be amazed	17
συνίστημι	unite, collect; introduce; show; prepare	16
ἀνθίστημι	oppose; resist	14
ἀφίστημι	cause to revolt; withdraw	14
ἐπίσταμαι	understand; know, be acquainted with	14
ἀποκαθίστημι	restore; bring back	8
προΐστημι	rule, direct; show concern for	8
ἐνίστημι	be here; happen now; be imminent	7
μεθίστημι	remove; turn away	5
περιΐστημι	stand around; avoid	4
διΐστημι	go away; go on; pass	3
ἐξανίστημι	raise up; stand up	3
ἐπανίστημι	rise up, rise in rebellion	2
ἀντικαθίστημι	oppose, resist	1
κατεφίσταμαι	rise up (against someone)	1
συνεφίστημι	join in an attack	1

καλέω

1 καλῶ

2 καλέσω

3 ἐκάλεσα

4 κέκληκα

5 κέκλημαι, κεκλῆσθαι (H)

6 ἐκλήθην, κληθῆναι (D)

Καλέω and compounds that share its principal parts:

καλέω	call; invite; summon	148
παρακαλέω	call to one's side; appeal to	109
ἐπικαλέω	call upon; give a surname	30
προσκαλέω	summon, call on, invite	29
συγκαλέω	summon	8
ἐγκαλέω	accuse	7
μετακαλέω	call to oneself, summon	4
ἀντικαλέω	invite in return	1
εἰσκαλέομαι	invite in	1
προκαλέω	provoke, challenge	1
συμπαρακαλέω	encourage together	1

καλύπτω

1 καλύπτω	4 (κεκάλυφα)
2 καλύψω	5 κεκάλυμμαι
3 ἐκάλυψα	6 -ἐκαλύφθην, -καλυφθῆναι (I)

Καλύπτω and compounds that share its principal parts:

ἀποκαλύπτω	reveal; disclose	26
καλύπτω	cover someone (up); hide	8
κατακαλύπτω	cover, veil	3
περικαλύπτω	cover, conceal	3
ἀνακαλύπτω	uncover, unveil	2
ἐπικαλύπτω	cover up	1
παρακαλύπτω	hide, conceal	1
συγκαλύπτω	conceal	1

κερδαίνω

1 (κερδαίνω)	4 (κεκέρδηκα)
2 κερδήσω	5 (κεκερδῆσθαι)
3 ἐκέρδησα, κερδῆσαι (H)	6 ἐκερδήθην
ἐκέρδανα, κερδᾶναι/κερδῆναι (H)	

Κερδαίνω (gain, avoid) has no compound forms in the NT.

κηρύσσω

1 κηρύσσω
2 (κηρύξω)
3 ἐκήρυξα, κηρύξαι [H]

4 (κεκήρυκα/κεκήρυχα)
5 (κεκήρυγμαι)
6 ἐκηρύχθην

Κηρύσσω and compounds that share its principal parts:

κηρύσσω	announce; proclaim aloud	61
προκηρύσσω	proclaim publicly	1

κόπτω

1 κόπτω
2 κόψω
3 ἔκοψα, κόψαι [H]

4 (κέκοφα)
5 (κέκομμαι)
6 -ἐκόπην

Κόπτω and compounds that share its principal parts:

ἐκκόπτω	cut off/down; exterminate	10
κόπτω	cut (off); beat	8
προσκόπτω	strike against; take/give offense	8
ἀποκόπτω	cut off	6
προκόπτω	be advanced; progress	6
ἐγκόπτω	hinder, thwart	5
κατακόπτω	lacerate; break in pieces	1

κρίνω

1 κρίνω
2 κρινῶ, κρινεῖν [H]
3 ἔκρινα, κρῖναι [D]

4 κέκρικα
5 κέκριμαι
6 ἐκρίθην, κριθῆναι [A]

Κρίνω and compounds that share its principal parts:

ἀποκρίνομαι	answer, reply; continue	231
κρίνω	select; judge, criticize	114
διακρίνω	separate; differentiate; evaluate	19
κατακρίνω	pronounce a sentence on	18
ἀνακρίνω	question; hear a case	16

συγκρίνω	combine; compare; explain	3
ἀνταποκρίνομαι	answer in return	2
ἐγκρίνω	classify	1
ἐπικρίνω	decide	1
συνυποκρίνομαι	join in hypocrisy	1
ὑποκρίνομαι	pretend, dissemble	1

-κτείνω

1 -κτείνω or -κτέννω
2 **-κτενῶ, -κτενεῖν** (J)
3 **-ἔκτεινα, -κτεῖναι** (D)
4 (-ἔκταγκα)
5 (-ἔκταμμαι)
6 **-ἐκτάνθην, -κτανθῆναι** (I)

Compounds that share the principal parts of -κτείνω:

| ἀποκτείνω | kill; eliminate | 74 |

κύπτω

1 -κύπτω
2 (κύψω)
3 **ἔκυψα, κύψαι** (J)
4 (κέκυφα)
5 –
6 –

Compounds that share the principal parts of -κύπτω:

παρακύπτω	take a look	5
ἀνακύπτω	stand erect; stand tall	4
κύπτω	bend (oneself) down	2
κατακύπτω	bend down	1
συγκύπτω	be bent over	1

λαμβάνω

1 λαμβάνω
2 **λήμψομαι, λήμψεσθαι** (G)
3 **ἔλαβον, λαβεῖν** (A)
4 εἴληφα
5 -εἴλημμαι
6 **-ἐλήμφθην, -λημφθῆναι** (J)

Λαμβάνω and compounds that share its principal parts:

λαμβάνω	take, take hold of; remove	258
παραλαμβάνω	take (to oneself); take over	49
ἐπιλαμβάνομαι	take hold of; arrest; catch	19
συλλαμβάνω	seize; catch; conceive	16
καταλαμβάνω	win, attain; catch up with	15
ἀναλαμβάνω	take up; adopt; take along	13
προσλαμβάνω	take, partake of; exploit	12
ἀπολαμβάνω	receive; recover; take away	10
μεταλαμβάνω	have a share in; receive	7
ὑπολαμβάνω	take up; reply; think	5
συμπαραλαμβάνω	take along with	4
ἀντιλαμβάνω	take part; practice; notice	3
προλαμβάνω	anticipate; detect	3
συναντιλαμβάνομαι	help	2
συμπεριλαμβάνω	embrace	1

λέγω

1 λέγω
2 -λέξω, -λέξειν or ἐρῶ, ἐρεῖν (D)
3 -ἔλεξα, -λέξαι (F)
   εἶπον (or εἶπα), εἰπεῖν (A)

4 εἴρηκα, εἰρηκέναι (F)
5 λέλεγμαι or εἴρημαι
6 -ἐλέχθην, -λεχθῆναι
   ἐρρέθην, ῥηθῆναι (F)

Compounds based on the various principal parts of λέγω:

λέγω (εἰπ)	say; speak; name	2353
ἐκλέγομαι (λεξα)	choose; gather	22
προλέγω (εἰπ)	tell in advance	15
διαλέγομαι (λεξα)	discuss, argue; inform	13
ἀντιλέγω (εἰπ)	speak against; oppose	11
συλλέγω (λεξα)	collect, gather	8
ἐπιλέγω (λεξα)	call/name; choose	2
παραλέγομαι	coast along	2
καταλέγω	select (for membership in a group)	1

λείπω

1 λείπω
2 -λείψω
3 -ἔλιπον, -λιπεῖν (F)

4 (λέλοιπα)
5 -λέλειμμαι
6 -ἐλείφθην

Λείπω and compounds that share its principal parts:

καταλείπω	leave (behind); leave to one side	24
ἐγκαταλείπω	leave; forsake	10
ἀπολείπω	leave behind; remain	7
λείπω	fall short; lack	6
ἐκλείπω	fail; depart; die out	4
περιλείπομαι	remain, be left behind	2
διαλείπω	stop, cease	1
ἐπιλείπω	fail	1
ὑπολείπω	leave remaining	1

μανθάνω

1 μανθάνω	4	μεμάθηκα
2 (μαθήσομαι)	5	–
3 ἔμαθον, μαθεῖν (H)	6	–

Μανθάνω and compounds that share its principal parts:

μανθάνω	learn; hear	25
καταμανθάνω	observe (well)	1

μένω

1 μένω	4	μεμένηκα
2 μενῶ	5	–
3 ἔμεινα, μεῖναι (D)	6	–

Μένω and compounds that share its principal parts:

μένω	remain, stay; wait for	118
ὑπομένω	remain/stay (behind); endure	17
ἐπιμένω	stay, remain; persevere	16
προσμένω	remain/stay with; remain longer	7
διαμένω	remain; live on	5
ἐμμένω	stay/remain (in); stand by	4
παραμένω	remain, stay (on)	4
ἀναμένω	wait for, expect	1
καταμένω	stay, live	1
περιμένω	wait for	1

μιμνήσκω

1 μιμνήσκω	4 (-μέμνηκα)
2 -μνήσω	5 μέμνημαι
3 -μνήσα	6 **μνήσθην, μνησθῆναι** (G)

Μιμνήσκω and compounds that share its principal parts:

μιμνήσκομαι	remember; make mention of someone	23
ὑπομιμνήσκω	remind; remember	7
ἀναμιμνήσκω	remind someone of something	6
ἐπαναμιμνήσκω	remind someone	1

νίπτω

1 νίπτω	4 –
2 (νίψομαι)	5 (νένιμμαι)
3 **ἔνιψα, νίψαι** (I)	6 (νιφήσεται)

Νίπτω and compounds that share its principal parts:

νίπτω	wash; wash feet	17
ἀπονίπτω	wash off, mid (for) oneself	1

ξηραίνω

1 ξηραίνω	4 (ἐξήραγκα)
2 (ξηρανῶ)	5 (ἐξήραμμαι)
3 ἐξήρανα	6 **ἐξηράνθην, ξηρανθῆναι** (J)

Ξηραίνω (dry, dry up; be paralyzed) has no compound forms in the NT.

οἶδα (ἰδ-/οἰδ-/εἰδ-)[2]

1 –	4 perf **οἶδα** pluperf **ᾔδειν** (B), infin **εἰδέναι** (B), fut perf εἰδήσω
2 (εἰδήσω)	5 –
3 (εἴδησα)	6 –

---

2   The stem εἰδ- is also used for the subjunctive, imperative, infinitive, participle, and pluperfect.

Οἶδα and compounds that share its principal parts:

| οἶδα | know; be able; understand | 318 |
| σύνοιδα | be privy to; be conscious of | 2 |

-ὄλλυμι

1 -ὄλλυμι
2 -ὀλῶ, -ὀλεῖν (H)
  -ὀλέσω, -ὀλέσειν (H)
3 -ὤλεσα, -ὀλέσαι (D)

4 -ὄλωλα
5 –
6 (-ὠλέσθην)

Compounds that share the principal parts of -ὄλλυμι:

| ἀπόλλυμι | ruin, mid perish; lose | 90 |
| συναπόλλυμι | destroy with | 1 |

ὀμνύω

1 ὀμνύω
2 (ὀμόσω)
3 ὤμοσα, ὀμόσαι or ὀμνύναι (G)

4 –
5 –
6 –

Ὀμνύω (swear, take an oath) has no compound forms in the NT.

ὁράω

1 ὁρῶ
2 ὄψομαι, ὄψεσθαι (E)
3 εἶδον (or εἶδα), ἰδεῖν (A)

4 ἑώρακα, ἑωρακέναι (E)
5 (ἑώραμαι or ὦμμαι)
6 ἑωράθην/ὡράθην, ὁραθῆναι
  ὤφθην, ὀφθῆναι (F)

Ὁράω and compounds that share its principal parts:

| ὁράω | trans: see, catch sight of; visit | |
| | intrans: look; pay attention | 454 |

προοράω	foresee; see previously	4
ἀφοράω	fix one's eyes; determine	2
ἐφοράω	gaze upon	2
συνοράω	become aware of; comprehend	2
καθοράω	perceive, notice	1
ὑπεροράω	despise; overlook	1

πάσχω

1 πάσχω	4 πέπονθα
2 (πείσομαι)	5 –
3 ἔπαθον, παθεῖν (F)	6 –

Πάσχω and compounds that share its principal parts:

πάσχω	experience someth. (pleasant);	
	be badly off; suffer	42
συμπάσχω	suffer with; have sympathy for	2
προπάσχω	suffer previously	1

πείθω

1 πείθω	4 πέποιθα, πεποιθέναι (H)
2 πείσω	5 πέπεισμαι
3 ἔπεισα	6 ἐπείσθην

Πείθω and compounds that share its principal parts:

| πείθω | convince; mislead; trust in | 52 |
| ἀναπείθω | induce | 1 |

πίμπλημι

1 (πίμπλημι)	4 (-πέπληκα)
2 (πλήσω)	5 (-πέπλησμαι)
3 ἔπλησα	6 ἐπλήσθην, πλησθῆναι (G)

Πίμπλημι (fill, fulfill; satiate) has no compound forms in the NT.

πίνω

1 πίνω   4 πέπωκα
2 πίομαι   5 (πέπομαι)
3 ἔπιον, πιεῖν [E]   6 -ἐπόθην

Πίνω and compounds that share its principal parts:

πίνω	drink	73
καταπίνω	swallow, swallow up	7
συμπίνω	drink with	1

πίπτω

1 πίπτω   4 πέπτωκα
2 πεσοῦμαι   5 –
3 ἔπεσον (or ἔπεσα), πεσεῖν [B]   6 (ἐπτώθην)

Πίπτω and compounds that share its principal parts:

πίπτω	fall	90
ἀναπίπτω	lie down; lean back	12
ἐπιπίπτω	fall on; befall	11
ἐκπίπτω	fall; drift off course; lose	10
προσπίπτω	fall down before; strike against	8
ἐμπίπτω	fall (in, into, among)	7
καταπίπτω	fall down	3
περιπίπτω	strike; fall in with	3
ἀντιπίπτω	resist; oppose	1
ἀποπίπτω	fall; deviate	1
παραπίπτω	fall away; commit apostasy	1
συμπίπτω	fall in; collapse	1

πλέω

1 πλέω   4 (πέπλευκα)
2 (πλεύσω)   5 –
3 -ἔπλευσα, -πλεῦσαι [J]   6 (ἐπλεύσθην or ἐπλύθην)

Πλέω and compounds that share its principal parts:

πλέω	travel by sea; sail	6
ἀποπλέω	sail away	4
ἐκπλέω	sail away	3
ὑποπλέω	sail under the lee of	2
διαπλέω	sail through	1
καταπλέω	sail down	1
παραπλέω	sail past	1

πράσσω

1 πράσσω
2 πράξω
3 ἔπραξα, πρᾶξαι [J]

4 πέπραχα
5 πέπραγμαι
6 (ἐπράχθην)

Πράσσω (do, accomplish; behave) has no compound forms in the NT.

σπείρω

1 σπείρω
2 (σπερῶ)
3 ἔσπειρα, σπεῖραι [J]

4 (ἔσπαρκα)
5 ἔσπαρμαι
6 ἐσπάρην, σπαρῆναι [J]

Σπείρω and compounds that share its principal parts:

σπείρω	sow seed; scatter	52
διασπείρω	scatter	3
ἐπισπείρω	sow afterward	1

στέλλω

1 στέλλω
2 -στελῶ
3 -ἔστειλα, -στεῖλαι [B]

4 -ἔσταλκα, -ἐσταλκέναι [J]
5 -ἔσταλμαι, -ἐστάλθαι [J]
6 -εστάλην

Στέλλω and compounds that share its principal parts:

ἀποστέλλω	send away/out	132
ἐξαποστέλλω	send away	13
διαστέλλω	order, give orders	8

ὑποστέλλω	draw back; avoid; keep silent about	4
ἐπιστέλλω	instruct by letter	3
καταστέλλω	restrain, settle	2
στέλλω	keep away; stand aloof	2
συστέλλω	limit, shorten; withdraw; cover	2
συναποστέλλω	send with	1

στρέφω

1 στρέφω	4 (ἔστροφα)
2 -στρέψω	5 -ἔστραμμαι
3 ἔστρεψα	6 ἐστράφην, στραφῆναι (F)

Στρέφω and compounds that share its principal parts:

ἐπιστρέφω	turn around, go back	36
ὑποστρέφω	turn back	35
στρέφω	turn; bring back; change	21
ἀναστρέφω	upset; stay, live; behave	9
ἀποστρέφω	turn away; reject; put back	9
διαστρέφω	deform; pervert; mislead	7
καταστρέφω	upset; destroy; turn away	2
μεταστρέφω	change, alter	2
συστρέφω	gather up; be gathered	2
ἐκστρέφω	turn aside, pervert	1

τάσσω

1 τάσσω	4 -τέταχα
2 -τάξω	5 τέταγμαι, τετάχθαι (J)
3 ἔταξα, τάξαι (E)	6 -ἐτάχθην, -ταχθῆναι
	-ἐτάγην, -ταγῆναι (J)

Τάσσω and compounds that share its principal parts:

ὑποτάσσω	subordinate; attach	38
διατάσσω	make arrangements; order	16
ἐπιτάσσω	order, command	10
τάσσω	arrange, put in place; order	8
προστάσσω	command; give instructions	7
ἀποτάσσω	say farewell; renounce	6

ἀντιτάσσω	oppose, resist	5
συντάσσω	order, direct; organize	3
ἀνατάσσομαι	organize in a series	1
ἐπιδιατάσσομαι	add a codicil	1

-τείνω

1 -τείνω	4 (-τέτακα)
2 -τενῶ	5 (-τέταμαι)
3 -ἔτεινα, -τεῖναι (I)	6 (-ἐτάθην)

Compounds that share the principal parts of -τείνω:

ἐκτείνω	stretch out; draw out at length	16
ἐπεκτείνομαι	stretch out; strain	1
παρατείνω	extend; prolong	1
προτείνω	stretch out; spread out	1
ὑπερεκτείνω	stretch out beyond	1

τελέω

1 τελέω	4 τετέλεκα
2 τελέσω	5 τετέλεσμαι
3 ἐτέλεσα, τελέσαι (H)	6 ἐτελέσθην, τελεσθῆναι (J)

Τελέω and compounds that share its principal parts:

τελέω	bring to an end; accomplish; pay	28
ἐπιτελέω	end; complete; fulfill	10
συντελέω	bring to an end; carry out	6
ἀποτελέω	bring to completion; perform	2
ἐκτελέω	finish	2
διατελέω	continue, remain	1

-τέλλω

1 -τέλλω	4 -τέταλκα
2 τελῶ	5 -τέταλμαι
3 -ἐτειλάμην, -τείλασθαι (H)	6 (-τάλθην)

Compounds that share the principal parts of -τέλλω:

ἐντέλλω	command; order	15
ἀνατέλλω	rise; be a descendant; shine brightly	9
ἐξανατέλλω	spring up	2

τίθημι

1	τίθημι	4	τέθεικα
2	**θήσω, θήσειν** (J)	5	τέθειμαι
3	**ἔθηκα** (D)	6	**ἐτέθην, τεθῆναι** (G)
	gen partic **θέντος**, infin **θεῖναι** (C)		

Τίθημι and compounds that share its principal parts:

τίθημι	lay, put; deposit; appoint	100
ἐπιτίθημι	lay/put upon; attack	39
παρατίθημι	set before; point out	19
προστίθημι	add; provide	18
ἀποτίθημι	take off; lay aside; put away	9
περιτίθημι	put/place around; grant	8
διατίθημι	decree; arrange; make a will	7
μετατίθημι	transfer; change; turn away	6
ἐκτίθημι	expose; explain	4
προτίθημι	display publicly; propose	3
συντίθημι	put/place wth; agree; decide	3
ἀνατίθημι	attribute; communicate	2
κατατίθημι	lay (down), place; grant	2
προσανατίθημι	add, contribute; consult with	2
ὑποτίθημι	lay down; make known	2
ἀντιδιατίθημι	oppose oneself; be opposed	1
συγκατατίθημι	agree with; consent to	1
συνεπιτίθημι	join (others) in an attack	1

-τρέπω

1	-τρέπω	4	(-τέτροφα)
2	(-τρέψω)	5	(-τέτραμμαι)
3	-ἔτρεψα	6	(-ἐτράφθην, -τραφθῆναι)
			-**ἐτράπην, -τραπῆναι** (J)

Compounds that share the principal parts of -τρέπω:

ἐπιτρέπω	allow, permit; instruct	18
ἐντρέπω	shame; have regard for	9
ἐκτρέπω	turn away; be dislocated	5
ἀνατρέπω	cause to fall; ruin	3
ἀποτρέπω	turn away from; avoid	1
μετατρέπω	turn around	1
περιτρέπω	turn	1
προτρέπω	urge (on), encourage	1

τρέχω

1 τρέχω	4 (δεδράμηκα)
2 (δραμοῦμαι)	5 –
3 **ἔδραμον, δραμεῖν** [H]	6 –

Τρέχω and compounds that share its principal parts:

τρέχω	run; exert oneself; progress	20
προστρέχω	run up (to)	3
συντρέχω	run together; go with; agree with	3
προτρέχω	run ahead	2
εἰστρέχω	run in	1
ἐπισυντρέχω	run together	1
κατατρέχω	run down	1
περιτρέχω	run/move around	1
ὑποτρέχω	run [or] sail under the lee of	1

τυγχάνω

1 τυγχάνω	4 τέτευχα
2 τεύξομαι	5 (τέτυγμαι or τέτευγμαι)
3 **ἔτυχον, τυχεῖν** [H]	6 (ἐτεύχθην or ἐτεύχθην)

Τυγχάνω and compounds that share its principal parts:

τυγχάνω	meet, attain; happen, turn out	12
ἐντυγχάνω	approach, appeal; pray	5
ἐπιτυγχάνω	obtain, attain to	5
παρατυγχάνω	happen to be near/present	1

| συντυγχάνω | meet, join | 1 |
| ὑπερεντυγχάνω | plead, intercede | 1 |

φαίνω

1	φαίνω	4	(πέφαγκα)
2	φανῶ	5	(πέφαμμαι)
3	ἔφανα	6	(ἐφάνθην, φανθῆναι)
			ἐφάνην, φανῆναι [I]

Φαίνω and compounds that share its principal parts:

φαίνω	shine; appear; be revealed	31
ἐπιφαίνω	show; give light to	4
ἀναφαίνω	light up, cause to appear; appear	2

φέρω

1	φέρω	4	-ἐνήνοχα
2	οἴσω	5	(ἐνήνεγμαι)
3	ἤνεγκα, ἐνέγκαι [C]	6	ἠνέχθην, ἐνεχθῆναι [J]

Φέρω and compounds that share its principal parts:

φέρω	carry, bear; produce; pass be moved; put	66
προσφέρω	bring; offer; meet	47
συμφέρω	bring together	15
διαφέρω	carry through; differ; be superior to	13
ἀναφέρω	take, lead; deliver; offer up	10
εἰσφέρω	bring in	8
ἐκφέρω	carry/bring out; produce	8
ἀποφέρω	carry/take away	6
καταφέρω	cast against; be brought into	4
παραφέρω	bring up; take/carry away	4
περιφέρω	carry about	3
ὑποφέρω	submit to; bear, bring, effect	3
ἐπιφέρω	bring, give; take to; inflict	2
προφέρω	bring forth, yield	2
παρεισφέρω	apply, bring to bear	1

φεύγω

1 φεύγω
2 φεύξομαι
3 ἔφυγον, φυγεῖν [F]

4 -πέφευγα
5 –
6 –

Φεύγω and compounds that share its principal parts:

φεύγω	flee; escape; vanish	29
ἐκφεύγω	run away; escape; shun	8
ἀποφεύγω	escape; avoid	3
καταφεύγω	flee; take refuge	2
διαφεύγω	escape	1

φημί

1 φημί, **ἔφη** imperf act indic 3/s (D)
2 (φήσω)
3 –

4 –
5 –
6 –

Φημί and compounds that share its principal parts:

φημί	say, affirm; mean	66
σύμφημι	concur, agree with	1

φυλάσσω

1 φυλάσσω
2 φυλάξω
3 **ἐφύλαξα, φυλάξαι** [I]

4 (πεφύλακα)
5 (πεφύλαγμαι)
6 (ἐφυλάχθην)

Φυλάσσω and compounds that share its principal parts:

φυλάσσω	watch; protect; avoid	31
διαφυλάσσω	guard, protect	1

χαίρω

1 χαίρω
2 (χαιρήσω)
3 (ἐχαίρησεν or ἔχαρον)

4 (κεχάρηκα)
5 (κεχάρημαι)
6 **ἐχάρην, χαρῆναι** [G]

Χαίρω and compounds that share its principal parts:

χαίρω	rejoice; greetings	74
συγχαίρω	rejoice with; congratulate	7

-χέω

1 -χέω
2 -χεῶ
3 **-ἔχεα, -χέαι** [I]

4 (-κέχυκα or κέχευκα)
5 -κέχυμαι
6 -εχύθην

Compounds that share the principal parts of -χέω:

ἐκχέω	pour out; dedicate oneself	16
συγχέω	confuse, stir up	5
καταχέω	pour out/over	2
ἐπιχέω	pour over; pour in	1

THE CONJUGATIONS
OF εἰμί, -εῖμι, AND -ἵημι

The verb εἰμί (be, exist) is well-rehearsed in all beginning courses. It is presented here both for the sake of reinforcing its paradigm and allowing it to stand in parallel with the verb εἶμι (I go, come), which is for its part familiar to students of Classical Greek but less so to most students of the Koine of the NT. The verb ἵημι (I release, let go) is known to beginning students of the NT in the compound form ἀφίημι, but it appears in other compounds, and some of its forms can be confused with the other two verbs listed here. It is worth seeing its paradigm in full. Forms found in the NT are bolded and numbered according to their occurrence.

✦

εἰμί

Indic		
Present	*Imperfect*	*Future*
εἰμί 140	ἤμην 15	ἔσομαι 13
εἶ 92	ἦς 6 / ἦσθα 8	ἔσῃ 8
ἐστί(ν) 897	ἦν 315	ἔσται 118
ἐσμέν 52	ἦμεν 8 / ἤμεθα 13	ἐσόμεθα 4
ἐστέ 92	ἦτε 10	ἔσεσθε 12
εἰσί(ν) 157	ἦσαν 95	ἔσονται 31

εἰμί

Subj	Opt	Impv	Infin
Present	*Present*	*Present*	*Present / Future*
ὦ 2	εἴην		εἶναι 124 / ἔσεσθαι 4
ᾖς 1	εἴης	ἴσθι 5	
ᾖ 43	εἴη 12	ἔστω 12 / ἤτω 2	
ὦμεν 3	εἶμεν / εἴημεν		
ἦτε 9	εἶτε / εἴητε	ἔστε	
ὦσι(ν) 11	εἶεν / εἴησαν	ἔστωσαν 2	

Partic		
	Present	*Future*
Masculine	ὤν 125 / ὄντος (gen)	
Feminine	οὖσα 24	
Neuter	ὄν 10	ἐσόμενον 1

-εἶμι

All forms of -εἶμι in the NT occur in compound forms. See page 36 in Part II above.

Indic	
Present	*Imperfect*
εἶμι	ᾖα / ᾔειν
εἶ	ᾔεισθα / ᾔεις
εἶσι(ν) 1	ᾔειν / **ᾔει** 2
ἴμεν	ᾖμεν
ἴτε	ᾖτε
-ἴᾱσι(ν)	ᾖσαν / **ᾔεσαν** 1

Subj	Opt	Impv	Infin
Present	*Present*	*Present*	*Present*
ἴω	ἴοιμι / ἰοίην		**ἰέναι** 3
ἴῃς	ἴοις	ἴθι	
ἴῃ	ἴοι	ἴτω	
ἴωμεν	ἴοιμεν		
ἴητε	ἴοιτε	ἴτε	
ἴωσιν	ἴοιεν	ἰόντων	

Partic	
	Present
Masculine	**ἰών** 2 / ἰόντος (gen)
Feminine	**ἰοῦσα** 5
Neut	ἰόν

-ἵημι

1st Principal Part

Present and Imperfect Active				
Indic	**Subj**	**Impv**	**Infin**	**Part**
Present				
ἵημι 2	ἱῶ		ἱέναι 8	ἱείς 4, ἱεῖσα 1, ἱέν 1
ἵης 1	ἱῇς	ἵει		
ἵησι(ν) 4	ἱῇ	ἱέτω 2		
ἵεμεν 1	ἱῶμεν			
ἵετε 4	ἱῆτε	ἵετε 3		
ἱᾶσι(ν) 3	ἱῶσι(ν) 2	ἱέντων		
Imperfect				
ἵην				
ἵεις				
ἵει 2				
ἵεμεν				
ἵετε				
ἵεσαν				

✦

-ἵημι

Present and Imperfect Middle/Passive			
Indic	**Impv**	**Infin**	**Part**
Present			
ἵεμαι		ἵεσθαι	ἱέμενος, η, ον
ἵεσαι	ἵεσο		
ἵεται 5	ἱέσθω		
ἱέμεθα			
ἵεσθε	ἵεσθε		
ἵενται 4	ἱέσθων		
Imperfect			
ἱέμην			
ἵεσο			
ἵετο			
ἱέμεθα			
ἵεσθε			
ἵεντο			

-ἵημι

2ⁿᵈ Principal Part

Future Active Indicative	Future Middle Indicative
ἥσω 2	ἥσομαι
ἥσεις 1	ἥσει / η
ἥσει 3	ἥσεται
ἥσομεν	ἡσόμεθα
ἥσετε	ἥσεσθα
ἥσουσι(ν) 2	ἥσονται

-ἵημι

3rd Principal Part

Aorist Active				
Indic	**Subj**	**Impv**	**Infin**	**Part**
ἧκα 1	ὧ 1		εἶναι 2	
ἧκας 1	ἧς	ἕς 15		
ἧκεν 20	ἧ 3	ἕτω		εἵς 21, εἷσα, ἕν
εἷμεν 3	ὧμεν 1			
εἷτε 2	ἧτε 7	ἕτε 11		
εἷσαν 10	ὧσι(ν) 2	ἕντων		

Aorist Middle			
Indic	**Impv**	**Infin**	**Partic**
εἵμην		ἕσθαι	ἕμενος, η, ον
εἷσο	οὗ		
εἷτο			
εἵμεθα			
εἷσθε	ἕσθε		
εἷντο			

-ἵημι

5th Principal Part

Perfect Mid/Pass Indicative	Perfect Mid/Pass Participle
εἶμαι	εἱμένος, **η** 1, ον
εἶσαι	
εἶται	
εἴμεθα	
εἶσθε	
εἶνται 6, always ἀφέωνται in the NT	

6th Principal Part

Future Passive Indicative	Aorist Passive Indicative	Aorist Passive Subjunctive
ἐθήσομαι	εἵθην	ἐθῶ
ἐθήσει/η	εἵθης	ἐθῇς
ἐθήσεται 12	**εἵθη** 1	**ἐθῇ** 1
ἐθησόμεθα	εἵθημεν	ἐθῶμεν
ἐθήσεσθα	εἵθητε	ἐθῆτε
ἐθήσονται	**εἵθησαν** 3	ἐθῶσι(ν)

THE PERFECT AND PLUPERFECT INDICATIVE AND THE OPTATIVE MOOD

The following three elements of morphology are often given light treatment in beginning courses. The aim here is not to give a thorough introduction but only a few tips that might aid reading.

PERFECT MIDDLE AND PASSIVE MUTE STEMS[1]

The perfect middle/passive inflection of λύω is straightforward:

	singular	plural	participle	infinitive
1	λέλυμαι	λελύμεθα	λελυμένος	λελύσθαι
2	λέλυσαι	λέλυσθε		
3	λέλυται	λέλυνται		

The 5th PP stems of several perfect (and pluperfect) middle/passive verbs end in a mute consonant—either labial (π, β, φ), dental (τ, δ, θ, including many that have a 1st PP ending in ζ), or palatal (κ, γ, χ, including many that have a 1st PP ending in σσ)—resulting in certain changes for the sake of euphony:

---

1. With thanks to the Wheaton College Greek 201 course materials of Douglas Penney; see also Alston H. Chase and Henry Phillips, Jr., *A New Introduction to Greek*, 3rd ed. (Cambridge, MA: Harvard University Press, 1941), 122–23; Stanley E. Porter, Jeffrey T. Reed, and Matthew Brook O'Donnell, *Fundamentals of New Testament Greek* (Grand Rapids: Eerdmans, 2010), 329–30.

Before μ:	a labial becomes μ	ἐπιγράφω > ἐπιγεγραμμένη
	a dental becomes σ	ἱματίζω > ἱματισμένον
	a palatal becomes γ	ἄρχω > ἦργμαι

Before σ:	a labial becomes ψ	λείπω > λέλειψαι (= πσ)
	a dental is dropped	ψεύδομαι > ἔψευσαι
	a palatal becomes ξ	φυλάσσω > πεφύλαξαι

Before τ:	a labial becomes π	γράφω > γέγραπται
	a dental becomes σ	πείθω > πέπεισται
	a palatal becomes κ	ἄρχω > ἦρκται

The 3/pl indicative endings beginning with -ν (νται, ντο) were avoided altogether by the use of the periphrastic construction (εἰμί + perfect middle/passive participle).

A σ between two consonants is dropped; so what would be τετριβσθαι becomes τετρῖφθαι (Mark 5:4); cf. ἀπηλλάχθαι (ἀπαλλάσσω).

The majority of perfect middle/passives are easily parsed by stem recognition (lexical form, PP #) and knowledge of the usual verb and participle endings.

PLUPERFECT

The pluperfect active = augment + 4th PP + ει + secondary endings:

	singular	plural
1	ἐλελύκειν	ἐλελύκειμεν
2	ἐλελύκεις	ἐλελύκειτε
3	ἐλελύκει	ἐλελύκεισαν

The pluperfect mid/pass = augment + 5th PP + secondary endings:

	singular	plural
1	ἐλελύμην	ἐλελύμεθα
2	ἐλέλυσο	ἐλέλυσθε
3	ἐλέλυτο	ἐλέλυνται

See above on 5th PP stems ending in a mute consonant. The augment is not always used, and there are other irregularities, but *if one recognizes the stem (lexical form, PP #) and a secondary ending, the parsing of most forms is straightforward. Note the ει connecting vowel in the active forms.* The most common pluperfect stems (ᾔδειν, εἱστήκειν) were included in the frequency list above. Not in that list but worth observing is ἐληλύθειν (ἔρχομαι).

OPTATIVE

Because there are fewer than 70 optatives in the NT and many of these are one of two forms (γένοιτο or εἴη, the 3/s of γίνομαι and εἰμί, respectively), this mood is probably given little attention in many introductory courses. Once one begins reading through the NT, however, those ~70 occurrences might seem less easy to ignore. Moreover, the optative occurs just under 600x in the LXX, over 120x in Job alone (17x in Job 3).

The optative occurs only in the present and aorist in the NT. The future optative occurs a few times in the LXX and also in non-biblical texts. The perfect occurs outside of biblical texts but is rare. Generally the perfect is formed periphrastically with the optative form of εἰμί and a perfect participle.

As with the other moods, it is wise to learn the optative endings and understand how the mood is built. The endings, combined with the thematic vowel and mood suffix, are these:

	Act			Mid/Pass
1/s	οιμι	or	ιην	οιμην
2/s	οις	or	ιης	οιο (σο)
3/s	οι (-)	or	ιη	οιτο
1/p	οιμεν	or	ιημεν	οιμεθα
2/p	οιτε	or	ιητε	οισθε
3/p	οιεν	or	ιησαν	οιντο

1. The initial -o- in the above forms is the thematic vowel. It is not used with thematic verbs (that is, ω verbs like λύω) in the 1st aorist forms of the 3rd PP or in the 6th PP aorist passive. -Μι verbs are athematic and therefore will never use the thematic vowel -o-.

2. The mood suffix is -ι- or -ιη-. In the act 3/pl, -ιε- is common before the ending -ν. It might be easier to think of the ending as -εν. The suffix -ιη- stands only before active endings.

3. The actual endings (distinct from the thematic vowel and mood suffix) are bolded. Aside from the 1/s -μι these are familiar *secondary* endings. The 1/s act can be either -μι (used with -ι-) or -ν (used with -ιη-). The 3/pl act can be either -εν (used with -ι-; see item #2 above) or -σαν (used with -ιη-). The -σ- drops in the 2/s of the m/p form.

4. Being a potential (non-indicative) mood, there is *no augment* in the aorist forms.

5. The 1st aorist 3/pl active sometimes uses the alternative form λύσειαν (1x in the NT).[2]

6. An alternative 2nd aor act 3/s form of δίδωμι is δῷη (4x in NT).[3]

7. The final αι and οι of the optative forms are *long*. While they can look similar, the 1st aor act 3/s *optative* can in most cases be distinguished from the 1st aor mid 2/s *imperative* and from the aor act *infinitive* by accent and/or context.

As always, parse by 1) lexical form, 2) PP #, 3) personal ending.

The mood is recognizable from the characteristic οι, αι, ω, ει *of its personal endings.*

The *present* attaches the endings listed above directly to the stem. There are no optative present tense contract verbs in the NT. The full paradigm of εἰμί is provided above (pp. 57–58); below is the present optative paradigm for thematic verbs. Bolded forms occur in the NT:

	Act	Mid/Pass
1/s	λύοιμι	**λυοίμην**
2/s	λύοις	λύοιο
3/s	**λύοι**	**λύοιτο**
1/p	λύοιμεν	λυοίμεθα
2/p	**λύοιτε**	λύοισθε
3/p	**λύοιεν**	**λύοιντο**

---

2. See Herbert W. Smyth, *Greek Grammar*, rev. Gordon M. Messing (Cambridge, MA: Harvard University Press, 1956), §461a. The explanation is probably just metathesis.

3. For explanation, see James H. Moulton and Wilbert F. Howard, *A Grammar of New Testament Greek.* Vol. 2, *Accidence and Word-Formation* (Edinburgh: T&T Clark, 1929), 83.

The *aorist* optative paradigm for thematic verbs follows. Here, λαμβάνω is used for the 2nd aorist active optative and γίνομαι for the 2nd aorist middle optative forms. Bolded forms occur in the NT:

	Act		Mid		Pass
1/s	λύσαιμι	λάβοιμι	**λυσαίμην**	**γενοίμην**	λυθείην
2/s	λύσαις	λάβοις	λύσαιο	γένοιο	λυθείης
3/s	**λύσαι**	**λάβοι**	λύσαιτο	**γένοιτο**	**λυθείη**
1/p	λύσαιμεν	λάβοιμεν	λυσαίμεθα	γενοίμεθα	λυθείημεν, -θεῖμεν
2/p	λύσαιτε	λάβοιτε	λύσαισθε	γένοισθε	λυθείητε, -θεῖτε
3/p	**λύσαιεν,** -σειαν	**λάβοιεν**	λύσαιντο	γένοιντο	λυθείησαν, -θεῖεν

TOWARD READING: A SELECT BIBLIOGRAPHY

In keeping with the aim of this Handy Guide as a resource for those who wish to engage in the consistent practice of reading Greek texts, a few additional resources can be mentioned. Such tools aid in the transition to advanced reading skill. The student is encouraged to search online for helps offered there (daily readings; supplementary courses; etc.). Further descriptions of all things listed here can also be found online.

GREEK NEW TESTAMENT

Burer, Michael H., and Jeffrey E. Miller. *A New Reader's Lexicon of the Greek New Testament*. Grand Rapids: Kregel, 2008. Similar to Kubo (below) but with updates, corrections, and additional information.

Goodrich, Richard J., and David Diewert. *A Summer Greek Reader: A Workbook for Maintaining Your Biblical Greek*. Grand Rapids: Zondervan, 2001. As the title indicates, this is a workbook containing a series of short Greek NT texts, helps for students with only a beginning knowledge of the language, parsing drills, lines for entering your translation, and an answer key in the back.

Goodrich, Richard J., and Albert L. Lukaszewski. *A Reader's Greek New Testament*. 3rd ed. Grand Rapids: Zondervan, 2015. This is a non-critical edition of the Greek NT sufficient for the exercise of reading. It footnotes the lexical forms of all words that occur less than 30x in the NT, with glosses. It does not do any parsing for the reader.

Kubo, Sakae. *A Reader's Greek–English Lexicon of the New Testament and A Beginner's Guide for the Translation of New Testament Greek*. Zondervan Greek Reference Series. Grand Rapids: Zondervan, 2015. In verse-by-verse format, this lists all vocabulary that occurs 50x or less: lexical form, gloss, and word count statistics. Each biblical book begins with a list of "special vocabulary," meaning words that occur less than 50x in the NT but 5x or more in that particular book. NT text not included.

Mounce, William. *A Graded Reader of Biblical Greek*. Grand Rapids: Zondervan, 1996. Another workbook with Greek texts and aids included. "Graded" means that it proceeds from easier to more challenging samples drawn predominantly from the NT, but concluding with two chapters from outside of the NT (Psalm 41 and the Didache). It closes with two appendices (summary of grammar; an introduction to "phrasing" a Greek passage).

SEPTUAGINT, CHURCH FATHERS, OTHER
HELLENISTIC READINGS

Decker, Rodney J. *Koine Greek Reader: Selections from the New Testament, Septuagint, and Early Christian Writers*. Grand Rapids: Kregel, 2007. This workbook is similar to the above.

Jobes, Karen, senior ed. *Discovering the Septuagint: A Guided Reader*. Grand Rapids; Kregel, 2016. This reader presents ten Greek texts from the Rahlfs—Hanhart Septuaginta edition. Explains syntax, grammar, and vocabulary of more than 700 verses from Old Testament texts representing a variety of genres, including the Psalms and the Prophets.

McLean, Bradley H. *Hellenistic and Biblical Greek: A Graduated Reader*. New York: Cambridge University Press, 2014. This includes canonical and non-canonical Christian texts, Septuagint (prose and poetry), Jewish Pseudepigrapha, inscriptions, and Jewish and Hellenistic literary Greek. Each passage of Greek is accompanied by grammatical support and vocabulary lists, as well as other aids to translation, including a cumulative glossary.

Wallace, Daniel, senior ed. *A Reader's Lexicon of the Apostolic Fathers*. Grand Rapids: Kregel, 2013. This is designed to be used alongside Michael Holmes's third edition of the *Apostolic Fathers* (Baker, 2007). It provides glosses of words that occur fewer than 30x in the NT, presented in the order in which they occur in the texts, along with the frequency of the word in the book.

Whitacre, Rodney A. *A Patristic Greek Reader*. Peabody: Hendrickson, 2007. Includes Greek texts, introductions, translation helps, translation key.

CLASSICAL

Balme, Maurice, and Gilbert Lawall, James Morwood. *Athenaze: In Introduction to Ancient Greek*. 2 vols. 3rd. ed. Oxford: OUP, 2015. This introduction to Classical Greek is a good second pass through a beginning course for someone who has already studied the Koine of the NT. Because such a student already possesses a solid foundation, this work can be done independently, though it will be best to have access to a tutor, and even better if the tutor has access to the supplementary teacher's manuals (obtained directly from the publisher). *Athenaze*'s many readings begin by assuming nothing more than the alphabet and advance in steps to unaltered excerpts of Classical texts, richly supplemented with historical and cultural sidebars.

Draper, P. A. *Iliad: Book I/Homer*. Ann Arbor: University of Michigan, 2002. A short but effective introduction to the Iliad and its Greek is followed by the Greek text with translation helps footnoted. This is not something to use right after one year of NT Greek, but it is well within reach of those who have gained some additional experience.

ALPHABETICAL INDEX OF VERB FORMS IN PARTS I AND II